T0158878

Mnemonic Verses

Mnemonic Verses

The Quest For Life
The Plague of Death
Remniscent On Mentors
- Pondering Over Love And Romance

Uchendu Precious Onuoha

MNEMONIC VERSES

iUniverse books may be ordered through booksellers or by contacting:

iUniverse
1663 Liberty Drive
Bloomington, IN 47403
www.iuniverse.com
1-800-Authors (1-800-288-4677)

ISBN: 978-1-5320-0269-4 (sc)
ISBN: 978-1-5320-0266-3 (e)

Library of Congress Control Number: 2016911430

Print information available on the last page.

iUniverse rev. date: 07/21/2016

Contents

FOREWORD

If one has ever met with the quest of life, when and where he had the first breath of life and thus became human, where then he goes therefrom, had thought of hands that reared him, of mind that lavished storge love on him, whence he is let to fly on his own without return for dinner like a baby eagle gone free.

What has he in his wings, mettle or weakling, courage or despondence?

Had ever wondered of love, achievements and means of accomplishment thereof that his sweat must accomplish. Imbue yourself with anthology of poems.

Desire direction of providence, acknowledge the mentors that you admire, learn from the exemplary and excel to the Olympian heights, then digest the anthology of poems.

To be a path finder, a maverick, a success in life, the 'golden tongued' wisdom in the anthology will nudge you through.

Dr. Clement Nduka
(Ikenga Nri)

PREFACE

Each person's life has a literary value. But these can only be harnessed if our life's activities and roles are articulated and penned down for others to know. Our world has missed a great deal of wise thoughts and literature from men both great and small, for lack of insufficient efforts geared towards extracting the thoughts and ideas that flow in the mind and preserved through writing and proper documentation.

My urge and motivation to write is derived from my interest to explore and dig deep into the wealth of knowledge, lessons and the beauty of our great universe which I see as a vast plantation with humanity as its arrays of crops offers. Some people talk better than they write, others write better than they talk. And our mind is a flow station where many thoughts flow.The world has produced and is filled with great men and women of great thoughts and ideas which sometimes are poured out in words through wonderful speeches, orations and dirges. The range of beautiful feelings that generate in our mind will not be meaningful if they are not expressed, put together, conveyed and preserved as a legacy for now and the future generation. Hence, I consider the great need to express the perception of my world,the great universe, and that of others in writing. Poetry is like a spell, when casted, it touches.

Mnemonic verses is an anthology of poems, prose, dirges, orations and reminiscent; composed and put together to form a great piece. These were derived from moments of interaction with self, evocations and reflections of thoughts and life during quite time. Also from romance with nature during visitations to sites and scenes of creation; messages received through muses of the mind; the serenity of messages heard from the quite, still voice during picnics to grave yards and resting place of the departed ones. Striking messages, orations and dirges put together from funerals of the dead ones. Soul travel to sea shores, mountains and valleys where no leg can tread, but only the soul in love with creation can reach. Messages obtained in solitary moments when the soul interacts with the unseen divine messengers.

The major theme among others is about death, mankind's worst enemy; an event that remains strange to man despite man's achievements and accomplishments. All things human are transitory and must cease or come to an end one day or another. Therefore, it's worthwhile and of much interest for me and mankind to ruminate our thoughts on death. Because, without being conscious of death, you cannot be fully cognizant or appreciative of the gift of life. Many people feel scared to talk or hear about death. But you cannot talk about life without death as they are like co-travelers, two extremes, identical twins and like two strange bed fellows they are. Where one ends, another begins.

This work touches on love, romance, and chastity. It is a creation and product from the mind's flow station processed, refined, and transmitted to the earth's platform for the consumption of the earthly dwellers.

As it is said, "A tree cannot make a forest, and no man is an island". I would be slapdash if I fail to acknowledge all the people who have in one way or another given me a helping hand and motivation, especially those whom their speeches, dirge or orations are mentioned and used in this work. Without your support and goodwill, I may not have come to this length. Above all, I thank the almighty God who is the source of wisdom and knowledge. He is my strength and in Him I trust. I thank Him for giving me life, material, spiritual and intellectual resources to pursue my goals.

Acknowledgements

This work is dedicated to my dear wife, Anthonia Nkiru and my beloved daughter, Annabel Ucheoma Uchendu for their abiding love, support and encouragement to me. For my two precious ladies, thank you for being there for me always. How sweet to be together as one in love.

To my most treasured parents, the late Elder Abraham Onuoha Nwosu. Papa, though you are gone, I thank you for your uprightness and the good virtues you imparted to me. And to my gracious and lovely mother, Agnes Nweke Onuoha, she lives on, Mama thank you for your wonderful love for me, your children and to everyone that comes across your way. Without people like you,we wouldn't have been. Mama for your love, the angels feel like orphans.

To my dear brothers and sisters, Elder Josiah Onuoha, Sarah C. Ajiere, Fineman, Florence Oluchi Edward and Glory Onuoha. Thank you all for your love and support. And to my in-laws, you are all unique.

To the late Dim, Odumegwu Emeka Ojukwu, the people's General, the late Ezeigbo Gburugburu and a hero I subscribe to his qualities and ideals. A man who sacrificed all that he had to defend his people. "Greater love has none than this,that one should lay down his life for his friends". Dim you are gone, but you live on. No sacrifice is too big enough to immortalize your name and legacies.

To her Excellency, Ambassador Bianca Ojukwu, the first ever Nigerian female ambassador to Spain. You are a great woman. The lives you impacted, your accomplishments, and the footprints you left in Spain will ever live to be remembered. I thank you for your encouragement and support. You are an ambassador and someone I will ever live to remember. Thank you for been my ambassador.

This work is dedicated to Ikoli Harcourt Whyte, a great man, one of the greatest inspirational Nigerian and African gospel singers, composers, poets and philosophers that ever lived. Though a leper, yet he did not allow his circumstance to limit him. A great man who sought a deeper meaning for his fate and proved that life has a greater purpose despite physical affliction. His voice and songs melted hearts and inspired souls. Harcourt White, if no one remembers you, I celebrate you today and I pay homage to you.

To my village Umuogele, I pay homage to you. A small enclave like the biblical Bethlehem. "Though thou be little among the clans of Judah, out of you will come for me one who will be ruler over Israel". You are the genesis of my life journey. Great Ogele, I salute you. In you will I sleep when my life has run its circle.

To the ancient Nri kingdom, for your historic significance to the Igbo nation and for finding my missing rib in you, I bow before you. My love for you will always remain. And to Dr.Clement Nduka (Ikenga Nri), a great son of the Nri kingdom, thank you for giving me a helping hand.

To all the old boys of the former Anglican Boys Grammar School Nbawsi, my Alma-mata, you know who you are; you remain the true friends I have. Thank you for your support.

Many thanks to Mr. Kelechi Amucha (Civigraphics) for providing the graphic images. And to my niece, Ms. Nkwachi Onuoha for providing assistance in editing of the manuscript.

It will be a remiss not to mention two great and worthy friends I found outside the shores of father land: Anita Thompson, my great Canadian friend. For Anita, " but there is a friend who sticks closer than a brother". And to Rafa Espinosa, my invaluable Spanish friend, "a friend in need is a friend indeed". I will never forget the vital role you played in my career.

To my opponents and detractors. "I have never in my life learned anything from any man who agreed with me" Unknown to you, you are a great asset to me. Rather than weakening me, you have given me strength. The harder you come, the higher I go. As a child of the universe, I abhor nourishing a hateful existence. "He who kicks a toad has given it a lift" Thank you for giving me a lift.

Above all, at this stage, I diminish and let the Omniscient increase and take all the glory.For without Him, I am nothing and cannot write if He doesn't give me the capability. To Him, I oweit all.

Part 1

THE QUEST FOR LIFE

BEES OF EASY VIRTUE

They swarm around men as bees .
around a calabash of palm-wine,
seeking for men whom to sell,
the dignity of their womanhood,
in exchange for mammon.
The treasure of Eve has been
desecrated by her daughters.
The virtue of womanhood
has become despicable
and her pride has become filthy.
Chastity has been thrown to the winds.

They belong to the family of dogs,
who, gripped by passion, openly
exhibit the animal tendency in them.
They go to sleep in the day time.
The coming of darkness
calls them to duty.
Their insanity begins
with the setting sun.

With ochre -coloured faces
and nakedness packaged
in tattooed bodies and dresses,
they lie in wait for their prey.
Some of their victims receive
painful stings that leave
their scars on them after time.

WHEN I COME AGAIN

When I come back to the world again,
I will be a vulture.
Because, the man I am offends me.
When I come again,
I will not be a hen,
a child bearer that reaps not
the benefits of motherhood.
I will not be a dog,
that vomits and eats those vomits.

When I come again,
I will not be a livestock,
whom its owner loves,
but when the day of feast comes,
he is killed and eaten up.
When I come again,
I will be a vulture.
The owner of the market.
I will have liberty more than man.

I will perch on top the house of
the great and small.
Food and livestock will I
carry without fear.
I will go everywhere like a king,
and nobody will hurt me.
When I come again,
I will be a vulture
I will have no friend or enemy.

If I Live Again

If I live again,
I will live like a blind.
Living not to see,
the scenes of sin.
I have sinned to see,
scenes of murder,
scenes of horror,
disaster and destruction.
Borne out of hatred
among mankind.

If I live again,
I will live like a cripple.
Crippling not to walk.

Like a snail,
crawling and creeping.
Not walking the paths
I have before walked,
paths of sorrow.

If I live again,
I will live like a deaf.
Having ears without hearing
the things I heard before.
Tales of liars, words of hate,
false rumors and gossips,
roaming through the ears of men.

If I live again,
I will live like a dumb.
Not speaking the things
spoken before.
Speaking no lies and
words that hurts.

If I live again,
I will live without knowledge.
knowing no right or wrong.

Why Mourn

In the morning of my arrival from
mother womb to mother earth, I cried.
While there were joy and jubilation,
to welcome my arrival.
What is the excitement and joy for?
I wondered, why I am here ?
And where am I going to?
My tender soul sought for
an answer from the celebrants,
none could give the answer.

The welcome has ended,
and the celebration is over.
The sun and star of my life are risen.
A journey to life unknown has begun.
Staring at me glaringly,
is the battle of life.

The battle to cross barriers
and jump over different hurdles.
In the thick of the struggle,
the greatest weapon
I possess is my will.

The will to a way and
the will to survive.
Firmly I cling to it.
Sometimes I am fagged,
but not fagged out.
Sometimes knocked down
and wounded but not out.
My will urges me to persist.
In this battle from different
angles, I am attacked.

My feet wobble,
and my strength wanes.
But my will stands firm,
urging me to fight on.
What is the battle for?
My soul ponders.
My mind knows not.
The cause is unknown to me 'cos
I was not there in the beginning
when it started.

The battle was raging on
before my arrival
from mother's womb,
and joining I must.
There is no escape, no retreat.
There is no going back,
for the border I passed through,
it's now closed.
And the boat that ferried me,
cannot take me back.

Now, I must fight on,
until night comes.
The day is half spent,
light will soon be
encompassed by darkness.
My day is far spent and
the sun will soon set.
There comes the night.
And here comes another
boat to take me.

I came through mother womb,
and I am going through mother earth.
Where I am going, I know not,
'cos I came not from there.
Now my sun has set.
In the morning were jubilants,
now gathered are mourners.

Mourning and wailing
for my departure.
Why mourn? when I am
no more in tears.

I cry no more,
for I cried in the morning.
In the morning, there was
laughter while I cried.
Why cry? Cry no more.
Why mourn? Mourn no more.
Where I am going,
you know not, 'cos
you have never been there.
Neither do you know
where I came from.

If you knew, you would have
told me in the morning
where the end will be.

Mourn no more for the unknown.
Where I am going need
no tears but joy.
Because it's a place of joy.
I see a better life ahead,
the battle is now over,
the struggles have ended,
am gone to the abode of bliss.
Why mourn?

Discovering Self

There comes a time in the life of
every man, both great and small,
to become cognizant of
himself and dispositions.
To the feeble minded, life is
a sequence of imitation and jealousy.
But to a great mind, there comes a time
in the life of every great man, when
he comes to the realization that
imitation is self-killing.

That jealousy is self-destruction.
That to be great, one must
prepare oneself
for better, for worse.
And should view that
as the two boundaries in life.

Though the world is
full of good orgies,
yet life is not an omelette.
No nurturing kernel can be cracked
for a man, except through his own effort.
Through his own hard work he must
toil, sweat and till his own vine yard.
Believe in yourself, for every soul
owes its existence to the tiny string.
Divine providence has allocated
to everyone a portion to cultivate on.
We may not all have the same smooth
and level ground or rocky terraces
allocated to us to
accomplish our life roles.

If you find your lot on the smooth
and level ground,
don't be complacent.
If yours is on a rocky terrace,
don't dwell on self-commiseration,
but try to recreate your own world.
The universe is a playing field,
you play your own wing
and I play my own wing.

Great men befriend their own self,
and believe in their own mind
to recreate their world to
the pattern approved

by their mind.
The reality of existence
is when one realize
that his world lies in his own palm
and he can mold and remold it to
any shape and pattern he chooses.

It is my fault if the world
does not smile on me.
Armed with this conviction,
I work assiduously to
subdue all obstacles
that may come my way.
Whoever must be great must
have a mind of his own and must
strive not to be a conformist.

He who would be
clothed with greatness
must not be circumscribed
by the name of goodness,
but must examine goodness
to see the virtue in it.
Nothing is greater than
the integrity of your own mind.
You may be misunderstood by many,
but remain courageous.

Great and good leaders of men
have always been mis-understood.
Absolve your conscience
from undue influence,
and you shall belong
to the hall of fame.

In My Own World

Strange is the world
I have lived to know.
The longer I live,
The stranger it seems to be.
Like a lonely wanderer
in the wilderness,
missing his direction.
Knowing not the path to follow,
I stop and pause,
and I ask myself a question.

Where am I heading to?
And where is my destination?
No answer could come.
In my confusion,
along the lonely highway,

I found two dwellers.
Two masters of the wilderness.
Religion and politics.
I embraced them

and followed them as
a sheep after a shepherd,
to take me to my destination.

They led me like a taskmaster
leading a slave.
Like an obedient child,
I followed.
Religion led me to a strange
path unknown.
Many sects and beliefs.
Christianity, Islam, Hinduism
Judaism, Buddhism and others.
Life after life.

No life after life.
The world will end by fire,
the world will not end by fire.
Trinity, three gods in one God,
no trinity, God is one.
Where do I go from there?
Not knowing the one to believe,
my confusion gave way to delusion.
In the conflicting doctrines
and arrays of religion,
I lost the more.

Politics took me in one hand,
and led me to another direction
with multi systems of rule.
Democracy, Aristocracy, Monarchy,
Communism among others.
In the splendor of power and might,
saying one thing and doing another.
With promise of heaven on earth.
Peace and security that never be.
Superiority of one race over another.
And one nation over another.

Racism and discrimination
in the human family.
In the path of politics,
I lost the more.
The masters of the art
have confused and misled me.
The answers and solutions sought for,
could not be found in them.
As a millipede recoils under threat,
I recoiled and retraced my steps.

Like a rebel, I chose to be
in my own world.
A world without religion
and God unknown.

A world without the
saintly robed priests,
a replica of painted grave.
A world without politics
and the gaudy mouthy politician.
I will know no priest and president.

I will know no religion and politics.
Not knowing no man or woman.
My relatives will be the
multicolored leopards,
Giraffes and peacocks.
The kites, doves and birds of the air.
Like a chameleon,
I will change color when I want.
I will soar like an eagle,
and to greater heights.

In space I would be.
In my wings, I will take
a flight to the moon
and to the outer space.
Like the great whales,
my habitation would be
in the mighty oceans.
The great mountains would
be my dwelling place.
My bed will be with the
bevy flowers of the garden.

Breathing the air of the
scent lily and rose flowers.
With the colorful and beautiful
Butterflies hovering over me.
The song birds will ever sing for me.
Death and life would
be my two seasons.
In summer, I would live in life.
And in winter, in death I would be.
In my own world I then shall be.

A Plea To The River

In respect, I come to you.
As a visitor, to you I come.
Strange you are to me,
and stranger I am to you.
I come not to live in you,
for I am not water-borne.
You are the only gateway
to my destination.
For a safe passage, I only plead.
Be kind to me as I pass through.

I am only passing by,
lie still, do not be rough.
Humbly, I appeal to you to be calm
and grant me a safe voyage.
Be benevolent to your guest.
I came in peace to you,
in peace let me go and return,
and bid me farewell to my origin.

BY THE CLIFF OF NINTH MILE

Across the steep of coal city,
I traverse.
Above the cliff, I ride.
By the forest of Miliken hill, I cross.
My destination is beyond the cliff of
Ninth mile.
Descending the cliff of Udi hill,
lies the Rope way.
Where I was caught with the beauty
Of the Ninth mile damsel.

THE NINTH MAN

In the beginning, God created Adam,
Adam gave birth to Africa,
Africa gave birth to Nigeria,
Nigeria gave birth to Abia,
Abia gave birth to Ngwa,
Ngwa gave birth to Nvosi,
Nvosi gave birth Umuogele,
Umuogele gave birth to Onuoha,
Onuoha gave birth to Uchendu,
And Uchendu became the Ninth man
In God's creation.

THE NEW PATH

Shrouded yesterday,
disappear like a blaze of smoke.
With your stumbling stumps,
thorns and tears.
Stingful bites and pains,
sorrows eaten up in a
hungry harmattan's fire.
Here walked upon for so long,
of many throbbing years,
with hopes dashed
and expectations flopped
with several near misses.

Lie buried and forgotten.
Wasting no time, I move on.
to a path never been.

Startled, I stop to watch and listen
to the sound of the wind.
And I hear the voice of a bird,
it whistles and says to me,
"move on, you are on the right path"
this long trail,
will soon meet with success.
I have chosen a golden high way,
I have found a new path.

Two Ways For Me

I have lived to leave yet I live.
I will live to leave yet I leave not.
I have lived to die but I live.
I will die to live but I die not.
Life is, and life will.
Death is, and death will.
Life was yesterday and now.
Death is tomorrow,
and time unknown.
Life will end when not ready.

Death will come when unwanted.
Unlike twins they are,
where one ends, another begins.
Life course is unknown.
Life must end at best prolonged.
Death must come at best postponed.
Today is, tomorrow will.

Life is present today,
and tomorrow may not.
I am not certain how today might end.

I live, for now the wholesome day
is not mine.
What comes next? I know not.
Life is a visitor,
it's not long to stay,
and permanent shall never be.
But surely must depart.
Today is, and now is.
Tomorrow is hazy,
and may not come for me.

How yesterday was lived,
I now remember.
But how my tomorrow
will end, I know not.
Time is, and time is not.
My lifetime is fast running.
Each tickling second of
the time clock,
clicks me nearer to the end.
Where the end will be, I know not.

But if I have a choice to make,
I choose to pass out
in the garden of omelettes,
Atop Mount Everest.
My funeral will not be by
the best of clergy or men.
But by flowers of the garden.
And the mountains,
Butterflies and birds of the air,
will mourn their guest.

Not on any ground
will my tomb be found.
But in the belly of an eagle,
resting at the uppermost
height above.
Until the resurrection morning,
before the ground
gives up her tenants,
I have flown to be with the Lord.

Part 2

THE PLAGUE OF DEATH

THE UNWELCOME GUEST

You are always on endless errands,
coming from an unknown
world and sender.
Like a thief at night,
you stole in unnoticed.
As swift as a scavenger
swoops to catch its prey,
you strike with the precision of
a fighter jet on a target,
to take your victims.

When will your snatching
fingers be tired?
and your cold feet
become weary?
You are without barrier,
and no wall can hold you off.
You have the master key
to unlock every door
of both the rich and poor,
the king, prince and princess.

Like captives and vanquished
soldiers in a battle,
all surrender before you.

Whenever you are around,
thick drops of tears,
sorrow, pain and loss
have always been
your parting gift.
Whichever door your
chilly hands knock at,
always receive an unusual parcel.

You always arrive
uninvited and unexpected.
No courtesy is acceptable
to accept.
No plea is pleasant to please .
Your departure is always
followed with tears and grief.

Strange and stranger you are.
When will you have pleasant
message for the bleeding souls?
your painful sting has stung.
Beware of my door, until
I hear of good tidings.
Your last visit to me left
bitter memories behind.

As painful as the sting of a scorpion,
the pains are felt
as the scars remain.

Please stay your
cold feet away from me.
Until you take me on a picnic,
and bring me back safely,
then will your message be a relief
and you will be welcomed.

MISTER DEATH

A cold wind,
a vehicle that doesn't ring bell,
a thief, a parcel everyone must receive.
Death, you awake everybody from sleep,
you cause turmoil in the city.
When you hold a hero on the ground,
it's like where a woman is held.
A blind that doesn't see,
a respecter of no one.
Death, you put an ocean of
tears in the eyes of men.

Terror to the ruler,
comfort to the suffering man.
You harvest the farm crops
whenever you want,
and wherever you like
from both big and small.

You snatch away from children,
their parents by force.
You pluck off from a widow, her only eye.
You are the killer of a warrior.

You knock off the pillar of the house,
and you knock down
the bricks of the house.
A criminal, a terror to everyone,
I hate you.
You think that you are cheating men,
Without knowing that
you are sending them to a place of rest.
Death, you are like a snail,
who thought that it was quenching the fire,
but killed itself.

THE CRIES OF A SOLDIER

Now I am in the battle front,
I know what lay ahead of me.
It is my death.
I hate not those I am fighting against,
but their actions I hate.
Those I am fighting for, love me not.
My death may not embitter them,
neither would it bring joy to them.
No law compels me to this fight,
and nobody obligated me,
more than the love I have for my people.
My friends want me to withdraw
from the battle front,
so that I would not die in the battle.
But they forget that a snake does not
bite a child in the presence of the mother.

It's true that my mother,
siblings, friends and the beautiful lady
I wish to marry are worried about me,
but I will not leave the battle
to allow the enemy take them
captive in my presence.

I have left home to reside in the forest.
The hunter I am now, is
to kill my fellow man.
I am now a bush animal,
as to bring peace for my people.
I live by war.
Listen to the sound inside the forest where I am.
Leave, leave, is our morning's greeting.
Everybody, everybody is the music of my gun.
As the sound continues, I forget my life,
and use my gun to play string like a guitar.

When the shooting of gun stops,
I use my head to laugh.
When I turn around,
those that ate with me in the morning,
are now dead bodies.
I know that a day will be my turn.
I have seen my death.
One day, I will lie like my friends.
Here the vulture, insects
and different animals,
would have feast upon me.

My bones would be littered in the forest.
When the farmer clears the bush,
he would see my skull.
When he sets fire, I will be burnt.
When crops grow,
they will grow over my bones.
There would be no beautiful lady
to kiss me, because
the soil is never kissed.
That is how my life will end.

The eyes of my people will ever
be longing to see me.
The last we saw ourselves,
was before I left for the battle.
The next we shall see, will be in the
kingdom of heaven.

MESSAGE OF A DYING SOLDIER

When you go home,
tell them of us and say;
For your tomorrow,
we gave our today.

Part 3

REMINISCENT ON MENTORS

THE HISTORIC DECLARATION

Having mandated me to proclaim on your behalf, and in your name, that Eastern Nigeria be a sovereign independent Republic, now, therefore I, Lieutenant Colonel Chukwuemeka Odumegwu-Ojukwu, Military Governor of Eastern Nigeria, by virtue of the authority, and pursuant to the principles recited above, do hereby solemnly proclaim that the territory and region known as and called Eastern Nigeria together with her continental shelf and territorial waters, shall, henceforth, be an independent sovereign state of the name and title of The Republic of Biafra...

The Voice Of A Hero

For you, I abandoned all ease
and embraced pain.
For you, I impoverished myself
to buy your protection.
Because of you, I fought
a three-year bitter war.
For you, I walked every battlefront
to assure your welfare.
For you, I stood when
every other person crouched.

For you, I endured thirteen
years of bitter exile.
For you, I endured ten months
of maximum security prison.

For you, I endured priestly poverty.
For you, I continue to struggle.
What I have said is not harsh,
it is only the naked truth.
And it reflects only the intensity
of the truth I harbor for my people.
Ndigbo, I have paid my dues.

A Hero's Dirge (Bianca Ojukwu)

How do I sum up 23 years in one page? I don't know. How do I describe you? I cannot. Not in any depth. Not for anybody else – you were my husband, my brother, my friend, my child. I was your queen, and it was an honour to have served you.

You were the lion of my history books, the leader of my nation when we faced extinction, the larger-than-life history come to my life – living, breathing legend. But unlike the history books, you defied all preconceptions. You made me cry from laughter with your jokes, many irreverent. You awed me with your wisdom. You melted my heart with your kindness. Your impeccable manners made Prince Charming a living reality. Your fearlessness made you the man I dreamt of all my life and your total lack of seeking public approval before speaking your mind separated you from mere mortals.

Every year that I spent with you was an adventure – no two days were the same. With you, I was finally able to soar on wings wider than the ocean. With you I was blessed with the best children God in heaven had to give. With you, I learnt to face the world without fear and learnt daily the things that matter most. Your disdain for money was novel – sometimes funny, other times quite alarming…

In mercy, God gave me a year to prepare for the inevitable. I could never have survived an instant departure. In mercy, God ensured that your final week on earth was spent only with me and that on your last day, you were back to your old self. I cannot but thank God for the joy of that final day – the jokes, the laughter, the songs. It was a lifetime packed into a few hours, filled with hope that many tomorrows would follow and that we would be home for Christmas. You deceived me. You were so emphatic that we would be going home. I did not know you meant a different home…

The swiftness of your departure remains shocking to me. You left on the day I least expected. But I cannot fight God. He owns your life and mine. I know that God called you home because every other time it seemed you were at death's door, you fought like the lion that God made you and always prevailed. In my eyes, even death was no match for you. But who can say 'no' to the Almighty God? You walked away with Him, going away with such peace that I can only bow to God's sovereignty. Your people have remembered. The warrior of our land has gone. The flags are lowered in your honour. Our hearts are laden with grief.

But I will trust that the living God who gave you to me will look after me and our children. Through my sadness, the memories will always shine bright and beautiful.

Adieu, my love,
My husband,
My lion...
You are a Hero.
God keep you.
We shall see after.

LESSONS FOR AFRICA

Christ came to His people,
but His own people
did not receive him.
The Jews saw a thief
and condemned their savior to death.
But today, the Jews have regretted.

When Mbonu Ojike killed
the white man in him,
and put on African tradition
and culture like a cloth,
Nigeria did not see
The virtues in this man.
They did not understand
what he was saying.
But today Nigeria
has remembered Ojike.
When Lumumba wanted
to unite Congo,
Congo called him a mad man
and they joined with

Shombe and the Whites
to kill their own son.
Today, Congo remembers Lumumba.

When Nkrumah liberated Ghana,
and wanted the whole
Africa to be independent.
When he said that the only White man
he could trust is only a dead one,
Ghana did not understand.
Ghana forced their own son to exile,
and their father died in a foreign land.
Today, Ghana has
remembered their father.

Which ones would I say?
And which ones should I leave?
As it is to the Jews,
Nigeria, Congo, and Ghana,
the same it is in all Africa.
Africa, you remember the cook
only when the meal is finished.

BIANCA

The heavens bestowed you
with rectitude.
You were made in heaven and
delivered on earth.
The earth was lucky to have you.
You wore a crown of
beauty from heaven.
A great daughter of the universe.
You were sown as the sowers' seed,
and you fell on a good soil.

Born and raised by the rich
and a king.
Loved and was loved by a hero,
yet you wore grace and humility
like a cloth.

You wake up from sleep early,
having a mind of your own.
Defying all odds and opinions of men.
You took steps contrary
to many expectations,
but that which suited you most,
and charted a path for yourself.

Like your hero, you have
The same mindsets.
You changed general norms.
In the beginning,
a father's name and identity
overshadows his children.
But your case was different.
Rather than are you the daughter of...
Yours was, are you the father of ...
In marriage, the God of fertility
blessed you with a double portion.

You have all it takes to tower
above the daughters of Eve.
You were ordained
a star from creation.
You are like a gold fish,
and your presence in
the water cannot be hidden.
You are like a northern star,
whose resting qualities in
the firmament cannot be removed.

You are the star of your generation,
shining the light for others to follow.
Great Igbo Queen, Queen of Nigeria.
Great daughter of Africa,
and mother of a nation.
Because you were born,
you have a mission to be here.

There Lived A Man

He sprouts forth like a mustard tree,
bearing fruits and seeds
that were dispersed and sown in
lands beyond.
Like a sycamore tree, birds of the air
nested on his branches and
many creatures found comfort
under his shade.

There lived a man, like an eagle,
blessed with a soaring swiftness,
flew beyond our shores sowing
seeds of wisdom unfathomed
in the lands far beyond.

There lived a man,
who like a great Trojan,
traversed the world
with the pen as his mighty arrow.
Piercing the heart of men,
nations and generations
to come with trails of wisdom.

There lived a man,
who like the northern star,
whose light remains constant
and always will shine.
Beamed his light to illuminate
people and lands under
the cover of darkness.
There lived a man,
when things fell apart,
and was no longer at ease,
the arrow of God fell.

Here sleeps the man.
Things have fallen apart.
The calabash has broken.
The birds have gone to roost,
and the eagle has landed.
Chinua is at ease.

ANOTHER DAY FOR SARAH

So many years but yesterday,
a baby was born.
Mother's face beams with joy.
Pains and pangs of labour, over.
The baby child cries.
Pains and pangs of life
begins for a tendril.
Cheerful guests and celebrants gather
to welcome the newborn into the world.
Happy and cheerful, guests are
while the young celebrant cries.

Why crying when guests are happy?
The face of a strange world unknown,
scares and stares at her.
Yesterday you were sheltered from
toil and labour by motherwomb.

Today, you are at motherearth for
a journey on a path to life unknown.
The welcome is over,
birth celebrations have ceased,
guests are gone.

Life begins for a suckling baby.
What part follows?
And what path does she follow?
In a world and life unknown.
A life's path littered
with thorns and thistles.
The battle starts.
A struggle for survival in life follows,
and surely you must fight.
Like a soldier in a battle.

She plunges head long into the battle,
with two opponents
daily contesting her.
Sometimes you are
bruised and wounded,
but keeps on.
Often weak and tired,
but not tiring out.
Fagged but not fagged out.

Nothing remains the same in life.
Today, you are what
you were not yesterday.
The snorty toddler of yesterday,
off from the clutches
of mother's breasts,
now bestrides the world.
The baby girl of yesterday,
is today's woman and mother.

Today, another celebration
is on for Sarah.
Unlike yesterday, celebrant,
and guests are happy.
A changing world you are in.
Today is your day and you
have cause to celebrate
the beginning of a life journey.
Be happy and merry in it.

Smile, laugh like you
have never laughed before.
Dance as if this is your first.

Though life may not have been
the fiesta you came for,
but while you are here,
and there remains oil in your lamp,
And the light goes not dim.
While the sun has not set,
and the autumn leaves remain green,
feast like you have never feasted.
You may as well make feast.

HARD TO SAY GOODBYE

It's always hard for me to say
goodbye to someone
good like you.
Yes, apparently it is true,
you are leaving.
Though I knew a time
like this would come,
or at best postponed,
yet it's hard to say goodbye.
Somehow I know we'll
meet again in the great future.

But where and when, I don't know.
So until then, you're in my heart.
You are an Ambassador
I would prefer never to forget.
Rather than saying goodbye,
I would rather say
thank you for being
my Ambassador.

Part 4

PONDERING OVER LOVE AND ROMANCE

Torments Of Love

Ooh! my soul why unease?
My soul valves are punctured
and bleeding uncontrollably.
Ooh! what is happening to me?
Rain drops of emotions.
What could this be that pierces
my heart so deeply?
Hei! be a man, I tell myself.
Alas! the more manly I try to be,
The more helpless I become.

What is it that torments?
Who is this that rends
and bleeds my heart?
Love, you are armless,
yet, you hit harder than blows,

to subdue a man to mental
and physical tortures.
How long will this plague last?
Ooh! battered soul,
Who can save you from this torment?
If not Amagret.

UNBIND ME

Your departure has left me bound.
Like the flaring flames
of a hammarttan fire,
my emotions are stirred.
As the cloud changes
the bright face of the sky
before rainfall,
my pleasure like
the taste of a bitter cola
in the tongue has gone sour.

Ooh! my heart screams,
wondering in awe and thought.
Would you come back to me?
Would she ever my love be?

Torrents of questions,
flows further still.

What shall be the
outcome of that journey?
As the sunrise
declares the morning,
will it be the dark day
that will bury the adder?

How that journey
may change her nature.
How her affections might sway.
Lost in thought,
would it ever be the same again?
Ooh! Amagreat, my heart is bound.
My spirit is bound.
The man in me and my
pleasures are bound and as gloomy,
like the face of a rainy day.

Today looks gloomy
and hazy until your return.
I am looking forth to the
return of the Ninth mile
damsel of the ninth man.
Time seems to drag and days
are longer than usual.
Like a crab, time crawls
and moves slowly like a tortoise,
when one is waiting for a lover.

But the feeling of ecstasy,
erases the length of time
spent waiting for love.

Where are the birds of providence?
the divine messengers
that did errands
for the fathers of old.
I wish I had a third eye,
to see beyond human realms,
as to behold you wherever you are.
I pick up your picture,
staring at me is your image.
Speak to me image of my love.

Ooh!what a speechless
snapshot ogling at me.
I wish images had voice to speak,
to reassure me that it is well,
enliven my mood, and tell me
That she is for me.
Ooh! Great,my great love,
Unbind my soul.

THE OLD WOMAN

When an old woman gets older,
It appears no bride price
was paid on her.
When sweet wine finishes
From the raffia palm,
it becomes an old palm.
When a tiger breaks its leg,
the fox comes to demand its debt.
In her youth, she draws like okra.
She sparks like lightening in the sky.
She was appealing like a ripe banana.
But when old age arrives,
beauty fades away.

The woman you see now,
that looks like death,
that kills men.
With wrinkles and ribs exposed

like an old basket,
with deep sunken eyes,
like whom death chased,
has sometime
caused sleepless nights to young men.
Old grand woman,
I am not the cause of how you are.

When old bones are mentioned,
it appears it's for an old woman.
Rejoice old grandmother.
You are a complete woman.
Be courageous in your old age.
Rejoice grandmother,
the beauty of the clan.
Since nobody sees the beauty
that is in your face today,
I see the beauty that is in your face now.

THE LOVE I KNOW

That there is love and lovers,
is unknown to my soul.
But that there is a love
my heart is knitted to,
is the genesis of affection.
She sets the limit between
love and lovers.
As the mother deer
thirsts for water,
so does my soul pant for her.

She is the affection my heart
craves and cares for.
Together like twins
in the mother's womb,
so I long to be together
always with her.

As petals blossom and bond
in the bud of a flower,
so does my soul derive pleasure
when she is on board with me.

Among many wishful
wish and wishers,
she is the one I know
to love and love to know.
She is a compliment of my entirety.
Hating not to love
and loving never to hate.
As beauty is pleasant
to behold in the eyes,
likewise she is the apple of my soul.

A black beauty she is,
clothed in ebony by creator's design.
An embodiment of the African girl.
Oh! the love of my heart she is.
Say it loud and louder.
Proclaim it before peers and pals.
Declare it before rivals and foes.
Echo it before heaven and earth
that Precious love is great.
Great is the love I know.

MIRROW MY HEART

The weak minds drink blood for love.
They say it is a covenant of love.
I need no blood covenant to love you.
I drop no blood to win your heart.
Covenant is a bond for fear and doubt.
It unifies insincerity and it's
a yoke to conscience.
An enslavement of the soul
and living in bondage.
My heart rejects it.

Open my heart and see love.
I shed no blood to proof
You are dear to me.
My affection for you is transparent,
my conscience is my sacred constitution,

I bow to the dictates of it.
True love is not shrouded
with doubt and suspicion.
It is an open secret.

Mirror my heart,
I expect no blood proof
to believe you love me
and that I love you too,
As I believe in you.
My conscience is my great witness.
Mirror my heart and see love.

THE NRI DAMSEL

Ebony, dark, chocolate.
like the potters' clay,
mixed together by the great potter,
giving birth to a complete beauty.
A sleek frame statue with features
fittingly packaged by
the grand designer.
Like a tree with many branches,
bearing a budding beautiful body.
A charming smile with a sweet lip
encasing the snow white open teeth.

Like the lilies of a valley,
opening their petals to the
early morning sun.
A sweet voice,
never, ever heard of.

A voice that would make
the hardest of men
go to sleep like a baby.
Known, yet unknown.
Seen only but the shadow.

Nearer yet like a mirage-
Present but only in the mind.
Once together but just a sweet dream.
A dream yet to come true.
The Nri damsel,
my promised land soon to enter.
My precious jewel,
ever mine to be.

IF THERE BE

If there be joy,
let it be for my sweetheart.
If there be sorrow,
let it be for those unknown.
If there be fortune,
let it be for the ninth man.
If there be failure,
let it be for those
who never wish well.
If there be success, happiness
love and life,
let it be for Annabel.

TIMING TIME

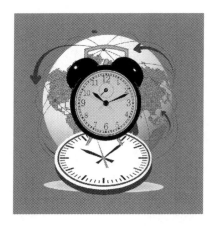

To everything under the sun,
there is a time, says the preacher.
But to everything that has time,
there is a time race
says the ninth man.
Time flies like a bird,
when sweet love is near.
And time crawls like a snail,
when Precious love is away.

Fly, fly and fly today,
for sweet love.
tomorrow will come.
Crawl, crawl and crawl,
tomorrow when
Precious love is come.

Wish You Had A Heart

Great ones master their thoughts
to assert their feelings.
Others without questioning,
accept uncomfortable thoughts
imposed on them to please others.
that is contradiction of self-freedom.
Yield not to that.
I do not welcome what you are
offering me in place of the
happiness we have
always shared together.

If you must abandon me, to
dabble into the hand of another,
compelled by your paternities,
then you have descended
from the high esteem

I have always held you in my heart.
If you ask me to go, I will go.
I will not strip myself of
the memories of you.
But I will leave my shadows behind.
For in the great future,
you may have a mind of your own.

MY SWEETHEART

If ever love was found in a woman,
Then you are.
If ever a woman was loved by a man,
you are the one.
If ever man is happy in a woman,
happier I am.
If ever two were in love,
then we are.
No woman, no love.

I value your love more than
all the rivers of oil.
Thy love I can in
no measure compare.
Your goodness,
I cannot comprehend.

In recompense, I give
my blessings to you.
Like a priest of the oracle,
I invoke and pray.

May the heavens
reward you hundred folds.
And like dews from above,
let the windows of heaven open
and pour its bounties on you.
Like rain drops, let the heavens
rain her love on you.
Hereafter, if two shall become one,
and together as one shall be,
surely, we would be.
That when we no more live,
we shall ever live.

Hard To Forget

How can I forget the first world ever lived?
The loveliest home lived in.
When my world was without form,
and the moon passed over me nine times.

How can I forget the motherwomb?
that gave me shelter.
The sun did not smite me by day
during the dry season.
And the scotchy winds and heat,
I did not feel during harmattan.
The rain did not beat me
during the rainy season.

How can I forget the breasts
that my mouth sucked from?
The most nourishing food ever eaten.
The milk that came from mother's breasts.

How can I forget the hands that fed me
when I was too tender ?
How can I forget the back that carried me
without a baby's trolley?
bearing my weight as
a camel would bear a load.

How can I forget the lullaby voice
that lured me to sleep?
You gave me shelter no one else could give.
You were my world when I knew no world.
Hard to forget you,
the love of a sweet mother.

References

1. www.shutterstock.com 27721573
2. www.shutterstock.com 110382677
3. Angel of Grief. www.pinterest.com
4. www.shutterstock.com 123240450
5. www.shutterstock.com 164409446
6. Biafra-guard.jpgsubsify.com
7. www.shutterstock.com 258271001
8. www.shutterstock.com 145273215
9. www.shutterstock.com 59111859
10. www.shutterstock.com 115251661
11. www.thinkstock.com. Getty images
12. www.shutterstock.com 171222647
13. www.blackpast.org/biafras-declaration-independence-1967
14. http://www.nairaland.com/816521/time-magazine-ojukwu-gentleman-rebel/2
15. https://nzesylva.wordpress.com/2012/03/02/bianca-ojukwus-tribute-to-her-husband-dim-emeka-ojukwu

Printed in the United States
By Bookmasters